A Very Special Christmas Celebration

By Noreen J. Floden

Illustrated by Madison M. O'Brien

A Very Special Christmas Celebration

Cover Design and Illustrations by Madison M O'Brien

The passing of a loved one doesn't have to be sad, you can keep their Spirit alive by celebrating their life and cherishing the memories.

Published in the United States of America.
Self-published by Noreen J Floden, McHenry, IL 60050

This story is dedicated to children who have lost a grandparent, relative, or someone they love before the Christmas holiday. May it give them comfort and peace!

The sky was gray with misty rain. The barren trees stood tall against the gloomy sky. Cars whizzed past with their back windows piled high with Christmas presents. I could see children coloring in the back seats of other cars. One Mom was eating an apple and the Dad looked intent on reading the road signs. I wondered if they were all going to their grandma's house like I was. It just didn't seem the same this year as it did in years before. Mom usually sang Christmas Carols along with the radio and Dad would drum the beat on the steering wheel. I always got a new box of crayons and a Christmas coloring book to keep me occupied during the long drive. I can color really well now.

But this year Mom was too upset to remember anything. So I just looked out of the window and sometimes looked for license plates from different states. Sometimes I counted cars of different colors. I knew that some things would be different since grandpa died, but
Christmas is still Christmas!

Poor Grandma! She is all alone and Mom said that she probably didn't even put up a Christmas tree. As I remembered the big, fresh tree and the smell of Christmas cookies baking in Grandma's kitchen, I began to feel really bad: no more homemade cookies, no more Christmas tree, NO more CHRISTMAS!

Before long I fell asleep slumped over the bucket seat with Rabbit, my stuffed bunny, in my arms. Rabbit always comforted me. He held my tears and wiped my nose when I cried. Even though some stuffing was peeking out of his foot and the seam was opening on his neck, he still was my number one friend.

I guess a long time had passed because when I awoke the night sky had replaced the clouds and the car felt cold. Dad turned up the heater a bit, but the cold air seemed to creep in through the cracks in the old van.

I closed my eyes and tried to remember Grandpa in his tan work shirt and his work boots, sitting in his oversized stuffed chair. I used to run and jump on him while he pretended that I was smothering him. This thought made me smile to myself.

Mom turned around and handed me a bunch of grapes.

"Eat these, Sara! It's late and grandma probably won't have much prepared."

So I took the grapes and a Christmas napkin and began to eat slowly. I only wished that Christmas could be the way it used to be. Why did Grandpa have to go to heaven now, I wondered? Couldn't God have waited until January to call him home to heaven?

As I wrapped up the grape seeds in my napkin I looked up and saw colored lights down the road.

Could that be Grandma's house? Why are there colored lights? As we reached the long country driveway I saw a big colorful tree that seemed to smile at me from the big picture window.

"Well, I never...!" exclaimed Mom.
"I never would have thought," exclaimed Dad.
"Look Mom, Grandma has a Christmas tree with pretty pink bows!

My heart began to feel excited again. When we stopped the car, Grandma came out with her blue Christmas dress on.

"Merry Christmas," she called. "Merry Christmas."

Mom and Dad looked at each other with a puzzled look.

"Hurry in before we all freeze," Grandma called.

Mom let me out first and I ran into Grandma's soft arms. Mom came next with two plastic bags filled with presents.

"MOM....,"she said in a questioning manner.

"Hurry...hurry...come on in. You'll catch your death of cold," she said.

Dad followed behind with suitcases.

"Come on Bruce," called Grandma, "Christmas is waiting."

Mom and Dad looked puzzled. Why is Grandma so happy? Didn't Grandpa just die a month ago? Grandma called to us. We all crowded into Grandma's kitchen that smelled like cinnamon and gingerbread cookies. Lights hung from the kitchen cabinets to make it look festive, just like when Grandpa was here.

"Well, grab a couple of cookies and let's go into the living room," Grandma said excitedly. I dashed into the bright living room and stood in awe at the magnificent tree that I had seen from the driveway.

"Come, come on in and see our tree," giggled Grandma.

"Oh Bruce, you know Grandpa's love of Christmas. Shortly before he died he bought all of these pink bows and asked me to tie them to the end of each branch. He wanted to remind you of all the good Christmas's past. He wanted us to celebrate, not morn his loss on Christmas. So each of you take a bow off of the tree before you leave. Take it home and put it on your tree to remember him whenever you see it."

Dad's eyes began to fill with tears, happy tears. Dad asked us all to sit down and he began to recall how he and Grandpa used to cut down the biggest tree at Old Doc's Farm. Then Mom told the story of meeting Grandpa for the first time and how she slid down the snowbank and knocked him off his feet. Everyone laughed and cried happy tears.

Just as I always did, I ran over to jump into Grandpa's chair like I had always done before, but Grandma swooped me up!

"Look at Grandpa's chair," she exclaimed. Grandma had placed a very, very large pink bow on his chair. Grandpa is here in spirit and wants us to celebrate.

Christmas **was** very special that year after all. Grandpa may have gone to heaven but his spirit was here with us that special Christmas.

The next morning couldn't come fast enough for me because we had the long ride home to see what Santa had left at our house. Dad played Christmas Carols on the radio and Mom harmonized. I sat in the back with Rabbit and the new baby doll that grandma had given to me. I grabbed the pink bow that Grandma had given me and tied it around Rabbits neck.

She explained to Rabbit, "It's okay to celebrate Christmas even though Grandpa is in heaven."

And Rabbit, wearing Grandpa's pink bow, made this a very special Christmas.

Noreen has many talents. She is a singer, musician, artist and an author. Since a young child, Noreen has always loved writing stories. Her vivid imagination and storytelling and wanting to help others, has now come to life through her many published stories. With the love and support of her family, her dream has come true.

Noreen is a mother of three grown sons, a retired Catholic school teacher, grandmother and a devoted Catholic.

She currently resides in McHenry, Illinois and can be reached at noreenstoryteller@gmail.com

Made in the USA
Monee, IL
21 September 2023

43031458R00019